GYM W

A FOOLPROOF GUIDE TO GYM EXCELLENCE

KEVIN HORAK

A CLOSE OBSERVATION OF HUMAN BEHAVIOUR

GYM WANKER

A FOOLPROOF GUIDE TO GYM EXCELLENCE

Published by:
Clearwater Publishing LTD
Netley Hall
Dorrington
Shrewsbury
Shropshire
SY5 7JZ
United Kingdom

CLEARWATER
PUBLISHING

Kevin Horak 2016
First Edition

ISBN 978-0-9557769-4-6

INTRODUCTION

The author has asserted his right to identify 60 different types of wankers that can be found worldwide within the gym; but there are many more wankers out there. In fact throughout our lives we will encounter some form of wanker every day - if you don't, you need to get out more as the planet is overpopulated with them.

The gym environment is a very strange place where we want to excel and become our best (for some reason) but it also has the habit of bringing out our very worst. So how am I qualified to write this critique of some of the strangest types of human behaviour?

Well, over the last 30 years I've been in and out of gyms from my early days working for Weider Health and Fitness to becoming a personal trainer and I have managed two gyms. Throughout all of this time I've made very few gains and am guilty of 11 different types of wanky behaviour from the 60 listed, so I'm a very disappointing level 3 wanker. A tick box has been added to each wanky style to assist you so you can work out how big a wanker you are after finishing reading this book.

To help you as the reader where you see this sign , I'm guilty of being this type of wanker.

This is my only qualification for writing this in-depth and highly informative guide. There are some wanky levels detailed within this book that I've tried to achieve but regrettably failed – some people are just bigger wankers than others.

These days I'm happily engaged to Lauren (Chilli Chapel) and I'm regularly observed talking to her in the gym. Unless I get banned for writing this book.

Couples wanker 3/10

If you feel that the author should consider other types of wankers for the future please email him at wanker@gymwanker.com, also please visit us at GYMWANKER.COM and become part of the community!

: Gymwankker
: Gymwankerbook
: Gym_wanker

So how much of a gym wanker are you? This wankerbility scale will offer you some guidelines. After reading this educational guide of gym wankers you will be able to determine exactly what level of wanker you are and exactly where you want to be.........or not to be – that is indeed the question.

Are you a low level amateur wanker or maximum level 10 wanker?

WANKER GRADING LEVEL

The Wanker scale 1-10 (10 being professional wanker status)

60 WANKER POINTS ARE ADDRESSED WITHIN THIS BOOK, IF YOU THINK YOU SCORE ALL 60 YOU ARE A LYING WANKER OR YOU HAVE ISSUES WANKER. IF YOU SCORE 50 OR OVER YOU ARE A LEVEL 10 CLASS WANKER, IN FACT THAT MAKES YOU THE BLACK BELT OF WANKERABILITY, A LIVING WANKOSAUROUS; IF SO PLEASE DO WRITE TO ME AT GYMWANKER.COM I WANT TO HEAR FROM YOU (PROBABLY), ALTHOUGH I DON'T WANT YOU IN MY LIFE.

Wanker Grading Level

Wanker Grading Level	Score
LEVEL 1 – AMATEUR WANKER	5 OR UNDER
LEVEL 2 – VIAGRA NEEDED WANKER	10 OR UNDER
LEVEL 3 – LONG WAY TO GO WANKER	15 OR UNDER
LEVEL 4 – MILD GAINS WANKER	20 OR UNDER
LEVEL 5 – GAINING RESPECT WANKER	25 OR UNDER
LEVEL 6 – DEDICATED WANKER	30 OR UNDER
LEVEL 7 – IMPRESSIVE WANKER	35 OR UNDER
LEVEL 8 – CONSIDERED WANKER	40 OR UNDER
LEVEL 9 – COLOSSAL WANKER	45 OR UNDER
LEVEL 10 – MAXIMUS WANKERMUS	50 OR OVER

DON'T FORGET, IN OFFERING YOU SUPPORT ESPECIALLY IF YOU ARE AN AMATEUR OR NERVOUS WANKER, THROUGHOUT THIS BOOK THIS SYMBOL IS USED WHERE THE AUTHOR IS A PROTAGONIST OF THIS TYPE OF WANKER BEHAVIOUR.

Legal Shit

Presumably you've bought this book as you have a sense of humour or you are buying it for someone who needs one.

This book is written around factual observations over years of not doing too much in the gym other than titting about. Although the author is a bit of a wanker he does not advise you to follow the steps here unless you wish to be a wanker and in doing so you the reader wanker accepts, understands and agrees that there can be consequences. If you pull a muscle trying to be bicep curls wanker – not my or the publisher's problem. At no point does the author recommend that you be bench press wanker and get yourself trapped on a bench. If you fly off the back of a machine trying to be a very fast wanker then you are simply just that, a very fast wanker. If you think observations written here are recommendations then you are a very stupid wanker so if you are considering being a legal action wanker because your nuts got trapped trying to be short shorts wanker or trying to be any other wanker for that matter you are a sad wanker and the author or publisher are not responsible. So get back to training as those gains won't come just by thinking about it!

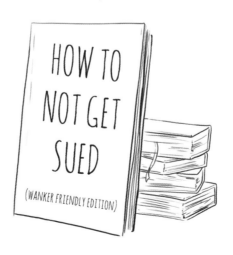

9

Observations Of Wanker Behaviour

Chapter 1: In the Gym, Gym Wankers

Chapter 2: In the Gym, The Style Wankers

Chapter 3, Commercial Chain Gym Wankers

Chapter 4, Changing Room Wankers

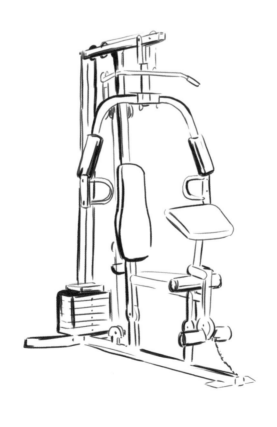

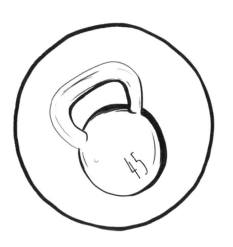

WANK CHAPTER 1
IN THE GYM, GYM WANKERS

1. Yelling and grunting wanker

Now when you've nailed that double dose of pre-workout and buzzing off your tits you want to make sure this workout you are going to boss, in fact you're going all out beast mode.

So the occasional grunt/groan/fart is entirely acceptable; although if you let the gas fly be prepared for gear wanker to go "there goes the protein" upon release of said gas. This is a mandatory statement in gyms, like a barman dropping a glass and some douche with original hilarity who says "sack the juggler". Juggler wanker is annoying human being wanker or often called no friends wanker.

So you're in the zone and hitting it big time, you ain't leaving until you've been sick at least twice, cardio can piss right off, this is deadlift/shoulder press or bench press day.

Now if you are training in a bodybuilding or powerlifting gym then mandatory yelling and farting is commonplace, in fact it's etiquette and it's important to blend in but when you are going to engage beast mode and yelling at yourself in the mirror, punching yourself in your bodily places and throwing the weights around, keep a watch out for suited chain gym manager wanker as he asks you to calm down a little.

At the height of your euphoria be careful not to take him out as he tells you off as then you are in trouble wanker.

Yelling and grunting wanker 6/10 ☐
Assaulting suit manager wanker 1/10 (not recommended) ☐

2. Amateur bench press arm curl wanker

Ok so we all need to start somewhere and the gym can be an intimidating place for newbie's. However, irrespective of your lack of experience there are a couple of dead certs in the gym that you shouldn't really get wrong as an initial starting place.

Now, these 2 movements are not technically difficult so for the beginner on observation they can look at both of these bits of equipment and not be so intimidated. More technical equipment such as the squat rack (which you don't do –if you want to be a serious gym wanker you NEVER train legs) initially appear on first viewing as hard work so keep it simple. However, it's still possible to be a complete wanker with these two types of lift and these steps will clarify how you get max wank points:

The bench press

To look like an utter bell end wanker on the bench press for your first time in the gym you need to forget that an Olympic bar weighs 20kg alone – wankers do not know this. So best thing to do is add a couple of 20kg plates to each side as they don't look that heavy? Next don't have a spotter (someone to help you if you didn't know) or ask for one for fear of looking like a new type wanker and proceed to lift the bar off the supports.

Next, break sweat as it was heavier than you thought and with a very quick action you let the bar fall on your chest so you are pinned to the bench, it's important to get totally stuck so you have to either shout for help or tip the bar to one side so the plates fall off and then the bar flips to the other side so those plates come crashing off as well.

More advanced wanker techniques is to have a snap back on back to front so it falls off your face completely destroying your cool demeanour and if you really want to impress squeeze out an impressive but determined fart that doesn't smell so much but just to add presence – volume is key.

Let the folks know at the gym that you have arrived!

To complete this movement it's important to leave all of your plates on the floor as wankers never clear up gyms after themselves.

NO PAIN?
THEN WALK
WITH SHAME

Bench press Wanker 7/10 ☐
Adding snap back and farts 10/10 ☐

Standing arm curls wanker

Well you've seen Pumping Iron on Netflix or some such place and you've recognised that standing bicep curls does not look too difficult and besides gaining those guns is what it's all about right!?

However, despite the fact that it's not technically difficult there is still a premium opportunity to make yourself look like an utter no guns wanker.

Ok, this will take practice.

Firstly use the machine (cable cross, one side only of course) so people have to wait for you. To look the part on your early visits to the gym you need to blend in so invest in Hawaiian shorts and white socks that you can pull up as high as you can (trust me, everyone dresses like this) – you MUST wear a vest as the bad boys guns will need to be inspected immediately afterwards.

Select a medium range weight on the stack (full stack wanker is a different wank technique and you don't want to run before you can walk) and when you lift upwards with each repetition it's important that you arch your back and on the way down stick your butt out, lock your knees and go back and forth with your torso every time you lift (please inspect the wankergram below).

In doing so this movement intended for your biceps also works your back, butt, neck and nut sack (as they get squeezed). Ladies reading this may feel like they miss out on the last bit but that's not to say that you can still look a total wanker by adding an 'I've got beef' vest over your sports bra or other upper body wear; alternatively add headphones and sing 'Sweet Child Of Mine' or anything by Justin Bieber while performing the movement and indeed you will look like a utter wanker.

After the movement is completed it's vital that you do at least 20 sets to make sure that the biceps (the most important muscle group in the body) gets totally maxed out, everything else is secondary. Afterwards do a pose off (with yourself) and show that blood burning in action.

Then leave the gym, your work here is done.

WANKER RATING 3/10 ☐
ADD SWEET CHILD OF MINE VOCALS 10/10 ☐

3. Full stack wanker

The full stack wanker is often not an accomplished lifter. Full stack wanker prefers to use machines instead of free weights and enjoys the mental victory of 'maxing out'. This is like a gym version of alpha peacocking and upon completion of your triceps push down, you stand back from the machine and lift your back as much as you can to give that 'V' shape and bringing out those triceps you have desperately just earned. Preferable bolt on skills include a little forehead sweat and after the 'V' put hands on hips and hope that someone saw you, now you can breathe out. Awesome good effort!

Wanker Rating 2/10 ☐

4. Front double guns wanker

This is an interesting type of wanker as they usually come in two forms.

1. Those who have trained
2. Those who have not

For those who have trained and are a competitive athlete – you have earned the right to front double guns and actually yes, we do want to see them (in measured doses thank you). But a professional bodybuilder generally does not make the habit of walking up behind people (usually more of a male trait than females) and presenting the front double guns for no reason and then just walks off, that's just odd wanker behaviour.

If they do throw a pose usually combinations are offered as well if they are in pre-competition form (for the amateur wanker, a competitor is not a wanker generally speaking as they have earned the right to show front double guns, unless they are a posing wanker with no excuse and just showing off and then they are a wanker like everyone else.....if you follow me?).

For those of you new or newish to gym testosterone, this behaviour is a little predatory like you are marking your territory, the front double guns is a showing of masculinity; for the ladies who do it it's like the sand is still being kicked in your face.

If you are a newbie and going to attempt this, to gain points on the gym wanker scale the most important thing is firstly to select a mirror where people are watching, this is very important. Make sure the mirror is ideally where the lighting is slightly offset offering the best definition. Once you are comfortable and ready, hit those guns and show your gym prowess, make sure people see you and then grab a selfie. Everyone wants to see the double guns especially your 10 followers on social media.

Sweet!

Wanker rating 7/10

5. Singing and whistling wanker

Why does this happen exactly? At what point do you want to hear someone walking behind you singing tunes, even more confusing when they don't have headphones on, what goes on in this type of wankers mind?

If we want to hear someone sing we go to a show or switch some tunes on, unfortunately this type of wanker does not have an off switch. Unless you are prepared (and some would say quite rightly) to become shut up wanker, if not, this can be a very painful gym experience.

The whistling wanker is even worse because very often there is no tune and they walk around making some senseless bit of blather up. Often a cross between opera/classical and drum and bass the whistling wanker is a twat of a wanker.

Singing wanker 7/10 ☐
Whistling wanker 9/10 ☐
Using the term "shut up gym wanker" 10/10 ☐

6. The Very Fast Wanker

Now this is one of those types that do cardio in the gym but not every day so they make the most of it when they are there – they are probably an over pressurised (w)banker or something. The very fast wanker is on a treadmill or usually the noisiest machine they can find and try to run a marathon in an hour.

Most of us are too busy to be Usain Bolt or Mo Farrah but when you get the opportunity, well you know, you gotta try right?

Facts with being a very fast wanker include:

- Sweat heavily; in fact run so fast that the sweat leaves you at such propulsion that people walking past the machine get hit with your shit like acid rain
- Breathe heavily (so everyone can hear you), perfect for attention seekers
- Get very red in the face and make sure you screw your face up with absolute determination
- For fast lady wankers make sure you invest in a good sports bra otherwise you are a danger to yourself and others – the gym should be a safe place and boob accidents we can all do without

For the very fast wanker to score top points, lose your footing at max speed and flying straight off the back of the machine crashing into the weights stand or mirror behind you. After the amount of noise you've made there is no casual cool walk away from this.

Very Fast Wanker 4/10 ☐
Very Fast Flying Off Machine Wanker 9/10 ☐
Boobs flying that you give someone a black eye 10/10 ☐

25

7. Legs day wanker

Would you believe it that professional bodybuilders and athletes actually train their legs?? Who would have thought, that's hardly getting into the wanker spirit of it at all!

When you think the legs machines are there just for show there are some misguided folk that actually use them.

However there is a wanker's way of having a random leg day (just to say that you did it). Basically just train the quads (the front of the legs for uninitiated wankers), the rears are called hamstrings which is a stupid name in anyone's book so let's ignore them and the lower leg has calves that serve no purpose at all so we won't bother with those either.

Ok, so it's quads time wankers!

So there are only really a couple of moves of any interest for quads training and that is the squat (quite hard work) and the leg press (better because you can sit down).

For the squat take your time and focus as this pointless exercise does hurt, whoever said no pain no gain had issues and was probably certified as an insane wanker.

Ideally for your first (and only time) use a confusing contraption called a Smith machine (??) and at least if you collapse there are safety hooks to stop the weight falling on you (if you set them correctly).

Make sure you use:

1. A Belt.
2. Gloves.
3. Obtain a random gym wanker to take a picture of you to show you 'do legs.'
4. Put 20kg plates on the bar (lots of them in fact) and pose under the bar prior to lifting – amateurs will never know it's not actually you and that the machine is taking the weight.
5. Wear short shorts to check the quads and then you can talk to the ladies with short shorts wanker afterwards (although he probably won't introduce you to the ladies as you've just rifled his territory).

After at least 1 set of squats prepare for leg press; there is also something called a leg extension that was invented after 50 Shades Of Grey came out and it's nothing more than a kinky fad so don't bother with that either.

The leg press can sometimes be situated close to hamstrings exercise equipment (usually 1 machine only) if it is being used ignore the person next to you lying on their front doing leg curls, completely pointless when you can buy long shorts to cover these up.

Engaging the leg press is a relaxed exercise, you get to sit down and put your legs up, great if you've had a long day being an office wanker. Ensure your expensive pumps are in good proximity to your knees when you put your feet on the plate, don't put your feet too low on the plate or you'll end up walking like one of those aliens in that Charlie Sheen film from years ago when everyone was 'winning'. Gently press up and down and you're done!

Now more experienced gym wankers may actually ask their mate to sit on top of the leg press machine while they lift as well as filling the machine up with plates, this sometimes is performed by men to impress the other sex, this is often mistaken by ladies that you are in a relationship together – fair warning!

Mr Gray will see you now.

Legs Day wanker 4/10 ☐
(as it's not that much of an effort and largely pointless)

8. Slam the dumbbells wanker

If you really want to annoy everyone in the commercial chain gym then slam those dumbbells down hard!!

This never fails and whilst dumbbell wanker is completely oblivious to everyone around them and the tutts of disapproval from the cardio people it is your right to slam those bells down as hard as you can, I mean seriously did you see what I just did!!??

After doing so leave the dumbbells out for the gym staff to put away as they are too heavy to lift again, you've done the hard work and besides that's what they are there for. If you slam those bells you are indeed a gym wanker.

Slamming dumbbells wanker 6/10

9. Ladies Man wanker

Every gym has ladies man wanker, it's inevitable like if you have day you will have night. In fact there are now ladies only gyms, presumably to keep ladies man wankers away – surely this is the only reason girls??

So ladies wanker is not a professional pick up artist; no, outside of the gym he has no game whatsoever, he can only hold gym related conversations.

Ladies wanker can take a variety of forms but importantly he is confident and will not be an athlete by definition, in good shape – maybe, but not a training powerhouse, how can he be? He doesn't have the time as he spends 3 hours a day at the gym talking to ladies. In fact if you happen to go to leave at the same time you'll see him stall at the door on the way out as he has a fear of the outside and things not 'gym related'. He spends Christmas Day as a depressive individual and generally sleeps all day for the one day of the year that the gym doesn't open. So ladies gym wanker is confident, he won't wear too much, probably uses the sunbed rather than fake tan as he knows that fake tan wanker can make loads of mistakes and he's too skilled for that.

It does not matter what you are doing ladies, but he'll show up like a bad fart that drifts around you all day.

Full of compliments and charm, ladies wanker is a rare male predatory breed but you must be mindful of the fact that he will have a complete inability to focus on just you and he will always be looking around to see who he can wank around next; so enjoy the moment or otherwise tell him to go fuck himself.

Ladies Man wanker 9/10 ☐

10. Talking about conquests with ladies

This is not limited to one per gym like short shorts wanker and although there may be an alpha leader there will be many vying for the title such as is the male behaviour.

There are those that talk about this specialist subject and there are those who don't, but male gym folk are compelled to engage in this female object of the species conversation. Strangely it's not a young wanker thing either and there will be a combination of ages of men in wank conversation, the 40 and 50 something's will still chip in their bit to show they've still got their shit going on, although they probably have to insert that special blue tablet in their rectum to get things going.

Problem with this and often forgotten by the older gentlemen in conversation is that when speaking to 20 something's you are probably the age of their dad. This can be very uncomfortable for young overexcited lady loving gym wankers, mental pictures can be painful pictures.

When the alpha group engage in this conversation all training stops as if to compare notes – and in doing so lose track of their surroundings so everyone hears. The use of terminology to describe the female vagina becomes varied with some words confusing to the older members of the group as well as the younger ones. The word clitoris is never mentioned as none of this group has discovered it yet and it probably doesn't exist anyway so usually the conversation is short lived.........much like their performance.

And then training resumes.

Conquest wankers 10/10 ☐
Use of the word clitoris in conquest wanker conversation...(a what?) ☐

11. Posing Wanker

Well if you are a competitor the posing routine is highly important. In a competitive arena you want to get it right. In the commercial gym chain gaining admiration for your hard work and dieting dedication whilst posing in the mirror is unlikely........they will just think you're a posing wanker.

So this is not about the competitors, this is about the guy or girl whilst you're doing your thing who randomly pops up and front doubles guns in front of you – most disconcerting. If you ever have the misfortune to engage in 'conversation' it will always be about them. They may ask your name but that will be it and it will be quickly forgotten in any event. The rest is an ego rollercoaster about themselves and how good they are, don't ask a question about politics or religion or you'll get a look of such disdain that you are now being a wanker. This is an advanced level wanker reversal technique and you walk away feeling like a wanker when you were giving it out, you now are a massive fail wanker.

Posing Wanker 8/10 ☐
Reversal Wanker technique (on you, you are) 10/10 ☐

12. Punch bag wanker

So you're not a boxer or martial artist and you've joined the fitness gym instead?

If you want to hit or kick the crap out of the bag you are in the wrong gym and join fight club instead.....where you are allowed to talk about fight club, you probably didn't go there for fear of being hit, you good looking wanker.

The punch bag wanker is one who passes the punch bag and just cannot resist in hitting it in some way. Usually wearing headphones they are blissfully unaware of everyone around them getting pissed off with you for the amount of noise you're making.

If your intention is to flirt with the opposite sex then you show them what you can do and belt that bag as hard as you can and then offer eye contact with your intended. Be careful not to kick the bag and then make eye contact as the bag coming back your way knocking you out in a gym is frankly a flirting failure. If this happens to you and your 'friend' happens to film you, you may end up on gymwanker.com, you will live in infamy.

Be careful if you see the quiet never say anything guy and he walks past the bag and headbutt's it instead, keep away from him as he's nuts wanker.

Punch Bag Wanker 6/10 ☐
Getting knocked out by punch bag 10/10 ☐

13. Walking like He-Man wanker

This is the alpha male of the pack, a hunter gatherer, Thor wanker.

Now this person is not a competitive bodybuilder, this is an amateur in a small gym wanker. Vest or oversized clothing mandatory, growling/yelling mandatory, bench press mandatory and he probably runs the local doors and will bounce your ass out if you show him disrespect. He-Man Thor wanker will inevitably take gear (steroids for the uninitiated) and will talk about it all bloody day long, he is also likely to have smaller genitals than most men. Attention seeking he is the lad of the gym and the go to guy for life advice or having someone kneecapped.

He-Man wanker as a predatory animal does not like it at all when other alpha males show up at the gym, even more so if they have a bigger chest or from a bigger city. Whilst there may be inquisitive initial flirtation between the two species as they figure each other out, it always ends in tears and one will go crying home to mum.

He-Man Wanker 8/10 ☐

14. ARNOLD WANKER

The words 'Arnold' and 'Wanker' never ever go together so don't try, remember he killed the Predator – you didn't.

If you upset the big fella you are 1000/10 life wanker, take up golf instead ☐

15. The wankers wanker

Top dog wanker who holds court with the gym folk, this is the dietary and training expert (unqualified and certainly never competed) who will advise everyone about their training whether they asked for it or not. You're doing your lateral raises and he (it's usually a guy) will offer you some advice as to how to do it better – often followed by a look at me and throws a most muscular pose without being requested. These gym obsessed wankers are usually on day release from somewhere but now they want to talk to you and save you from making the mistakes you have been.

The wankers wanker will have plenty to say and often smiles, never frowns as they are doing you a favour, pay attention as what they learnt at the correctional facility is what they want to show you. The wankers wanker will have a following as he lays down the terms of how you get your life sorted, high fives standard and having to buy them a protein shake or smoking a joint with them afterwards is mandatory.

In every gym across the globe there is always someone wanting to offer you misguided advice that you never asked for – this is the wankers wanker.

The wankers wanker 8/10 ☐

16. Hung-over/vomiting wanker

So you booked your session with a personal trainer or someone bought you a session because they didn't really like you, but you decided to go out on the pop the night before and ended up getting wankered.

Against all expectations you actually had a good night, got laid and now you have the prospect of a very fit smiling personal trainer ready to talk to you and show you a healthy

LIFESTYLE FIRST THING THE NEXT MORNING. YOUR DISGRACEFUL CAREFREE/HEDONISTIC LIFESTYLE ALSO REMINDS YOU THAT YOU'VE NOT BEEN TO CHURCH FOR SOME TIME – SHAME ON YOU...............SHAME!

SO WHILST YOU'RE IN THE THROES OF PILING SO MANY ENERGY DRINKS DOWN YOUR THROAT SO YOU CAN WAKE UP TO GO AND BURN A FEW CALORIES (BUT JUST CONSUMED 1000) THE PROSPECT OF A SMILING FIT PERSONAL TRAINER IS NOT A GOOD ONE. BUT YOU KNOW YOU HAVE TO SHOW UP OR THEY JUST KEEP FUCKING RINGING YOU AND MAKE YOUR LIFE HELL. IF YOU ENGAGE A PERSONAL TRAINER AND DON'T SHOW UP, JUST MAKE SURE THEY DON'T HAVE YOUR HOME ADDRESS OR THEY WILL SHOW UP AT YOUR HOME AS WELL. FOR SOME REASON THEY NEVER SLEEP AND WHETHER YOU GO IN THE GYM AT 6AM OR 10PM THEY ARE ALWAYS THERE? IT'S LIKE THEY SHAPE SHIFT OR SOMETHING AND YOU CAN BET YOUR LIFE IF YOU SKIP A SESSION WITH THEM THEY WILL KNOW INSTANTLY AND WHERE TO FIND YOU AND YOUR HOME ADDRESS IS ONLY JUST A MATTER OF TIME. MOST PERSONAL TRAINERS ARE NOW SKILLED IN SURVEILLANCE, COMBATIVE FIGHT TECHNIQUES AND COVERT OPERATIONS AND THEY WILL FIND YOU SO YOU WILL REGRET THAT HANGOVER YOU UNHEALTHY DRUNKEN STONER WASTE OF SPACE!!

IF UPON ARRIVING AT THE GYM AND YOUR BREATHALYZER SAID THAT YOU CAN DRIVE IN THE FIRST PLACE? ITS BEST TO GET THE VOMIT OUT THE WAY AS SOON AS POSSIBLE - VOMITING IN THE GYM WANKER JUST ANNOYS EVERYONE; YOU REALLY SHOULD NOT HAVE DRUNK ABSINTHE LAST NIGHT SHOULD YOU?

SO WHILST PERSONAL TRAINER ATTENDS TO YOUR NEEDS ITS BEST TO SUGGEST THAT YOU DISCUSS YOUR NEEDS OVER A COFFEE OR IF THE GYM HAS IT, A GENTLE SWIM.

HUNG OVER WANKER 4/10 ☐
VOMITING IN GYM WANKER 10/10 ☐

17. Sweaty wanker

Firstly those posh speaking public school Brits that say that ladies do not sweat.....they perspire or glow; well that's utter bull in a gym at what feels like 100 degrees.

If you're a human toaster and you know you sweat it is not cool to leave your body dribble all over the machines or floor and the seats in the commercial bars after your workout as you celebrate with a pint for a job well done.

If you are a sweaty wanker the most important thing to really piss people off is do not have a towel at all or just carry a tiny flannel the size to wipe a babies butt.

To really finish off the look, wear shorts and a very small vest and hairy shoulders is a must, we all like to see the gleaming hairs as you walk round after your 20 minutes cardio and then lay flat on a bench and leave your sweaty silhouette behind like something out of a CSI murder scene.

To gain maximum Wank-Fu respect select a machine that is a seated upright such as an incline chest press and then you can leave your nut sack sweat imprint on the seat as well as your gleaming back and shoulder hair outline. Vitally important other than not having a towel is never use the mandatory wipes that commercial chain gyms say you should use every time you breeze by them – don't do this at all or you'll never be a qualified sweaty gym wanker.

Sweaty Wankerability level 6/10 ☐

18. Body Odour Wanker

Now this is an interesting type of wanker as they have an effect on everyone, the only person not affected and blissfully unaware is themselves.

In fact, if you are not in proximity you can observe as they enter the gym as they leave faces of horror behind them in their wake, usually completely oblivious to everyone moving rapidly away from them. If the BO wanker has headphones on others will usually cough or do vomit noises behind them. Very rarely is something said directly to them about their BO problem because that is bad etiquette right?

Its difficult scoring the BO wanker as to how they are such a wanker, how can you not know that you smell so bad unless you have some sort of nasal malfunction?

For organised gyms they are on hand with deodorants to assist BO wanker and they will be strategically placed for their use but they go completed unnoticed. BO wanker will often engage with sweaty wanker to talk about the football or some other mediocre alpha male subject matter.

Now for BO wanker to really gain wank respect it is of course not just about the smell, no, it's the look as well. Best thing is ALWAYS to wear white socks and as they take off those so loved pumps that they've worn since the 90's to do press ups revealing those white socks with black heels; preferably a little hole in the socks as well really completes this look.

Available for BO wanker, but never used.

Body odour wanker level 6/10 □
Add holes in socks 7/10 □

WANK CHAPTER 2
IN THE GYM, THE STYLE WANKERS

19. Short shorts wanker

One of the most disturbing sights in the gym is short shorts wanker. It makes everyone uncomfortable but yet most gyms have one.

Short shorts wanker will often be observed chatting to the ladies often propped against a cardio machine. He'll talk away while they are going for it and becoming more uncomfortable as the sweat (sorry perspiration) runs down their face. He never gets the hint to go and if he does exercise it's always a full body workout. Strangely the short shorts wanker does train legs as squat and leg pressing show the full flexibility of his shorts as they ride up his 'quads'. Short shorts wanker never suffers from embarrassment and will also be on hand to assist the ladies if they need a spotter. This is especially useful if they are doing bench press and he has to stand over them (with no underwear on).

Short shorts wanker has no qualms about the showing of his Johnson – God gave it to him.

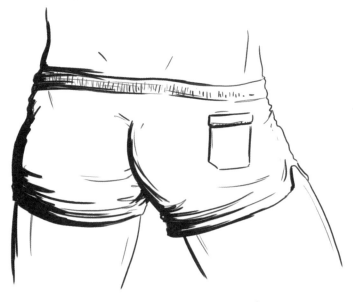

Short Shorts Wanker 9/10 ☐

20. Sunglasses Wanker

If you are training at Venice beach or you are Mr/Mrs. Olympia then you are excused.

If however you are indoors and don't have some form of eye condition and you show up to train with your shades on you are a masterclass wanker, in fact you are an off the planet wankernaught.

You've earned maximum points – congratulations.

MAVERICK'S TRAIN HERE

Sunglasses Wanker 10/10 ☐

21. Hat wanker

Ah yes, the hat wanker.

Now this is a rare breed and not found in every gym, you have to seek these out. A bit like Colin Farrell looking really cool wearing a huge beanie hat in the Los Angeles heat in the height of summer — that does look cool right?

The hat wanker is a complicated person and usually has more accompaniments than just the hat.

For some reason they often have shorts/training bottoms but with work boots on (usually dirty), they are often massive in appearance and always wear a vest. Fake tan is NOT optional and is a necessary part of completing the look; hats must never be snapbacks and must always be beanie/winter hats when it's the hottest time of the year.

Other hat wank efforts can include the wearing of a Stetson and that's John Wayne Wanker and a sombrero is a Mexican wanker.

To achieve maximum wank level hat wanker status you need to have more than just a hat, add the vest and work boots.

Full combination hat wanker 7/10 ☐
Full combination hat wanker in 100 degrees of heat 10/10 ☐

22. Oversize Clothing Wanker

Walking down the high street to buy your clothes like in the good old days before we all became internet wankers we never had a shop called 'Brick Shit House Clothing'; I know, I looked.

But they are out there somewhere because in every gym for years there is always someone wearing tops that the Hulk couldn't get out of. Now if you're a big guy/girl — cool, it's when someone wears those tops and bottoms that are realistically at least 5 sizes too big for you.

If you think you look cool — you don't.

If you have been making those gains and have suddenly gone up in size, XXL will not be sufficient any more, generally speaking you are looking for one of the following:

- Size Tent wanker
- Size Barn Door wanker
- Size Mammoth
- Size Tyrannosaurus wanker
- Size Everest wanker

Oversize clothing wanker 6/10

23. Fake tan wanker

Well we all like to look our best despite the pain we put ourselves through while gymming it; just think if you were not here you could be at the pub or having a social life or some such notion but seeing as you don't, let's go to the gym and look good instead.

Make up sorted, hair sorted, shoulder hair trimmed and perfume/aftershave on, you can't let yourself down at the final hurdle without looking like you've just come back from your weekend in Benidorm (no white tan lines please ladies and gents).

However newbie fake tan wankers will make mistakes and there is no forgiving for getting this wrong. Firstly be very careful how you use the tan around your face, elbows and knees, there is a prime opportunity for looking not so much as a gym wanker, more a complete twat of a bellend wanker. Get this wrong you are confined to the house for at least 3 months.

Also you may not be aware that you smell like a packet of biscuits and if someone next to you is carb deprived they may start dribbling around you. Bodybuilders and fitness competitors pre-competition can turn into vampire wankers without warning so hide the bloody biscuits smell or bloody it will get.

For the completely uninitiated who likes to carry a towel round with them – for God's sake if it's white never use it! The towel is for show only; a little bit of sweat and you rub that on your crisp white towel and before you know it you're walking around with a massive shit stain in your hands; a combination of your towel looking like its covered in pump action protein whilst you smell of biscuits will earn you a wanker level rating higher than smelly wanker.

If you decide to go to the spa or sauna afterwards just bear in mind that the water can change colour quickly and also your biscuit dribble can go all over the floor.

MAKE UP

PERFECT HAIR

MELTING LIKE THE WICKED WITCH

SMELLS LIKE BISCUITS

SHIT STAINED TOWEL

Fake tan Wanker 6/10 ☐
Carrying around a shit stained towel 8/10 ☐
Dying the colour of the spa water 9/10 ☐
Surviving vampire wanker (it's never happened)

24. Trendy Tattoo Wanker

To be the maximum trendy tattoo wanker there are some very basic principles that need to be followed.

Firstly you need to have no interest in tattoos whatsoever; you did this just as a fashion statement.

To qualify for this you need to have a full sleeve tattoo but ONLY 1 arm – never do both as you've then moved on from trendy tattoo wanker and may actually like tattoos – this is not cool in the gym if your intention is to be a wanker.

Also you must not do ANY research on tattoos at all and ensure that you have exactly the same as everyone else, don't use any originality at all and most definitely not your own ideas, usually stars, flowers, skulls and tribal symbols that you have no idea what they mean would be perfect to ensure your wanker level status.

Ladies – if your tramp stamp has faded you can join this club.

If you are concerned that you may have fallen into this wanker category and if you are offended you could always add love/hate across your knuckles – then you're a hard wanker.

Trendy Tattoo Wanker 9/10 □

25. Jeans wanker

For some reason there are still a few individuals that think jeans in the gym is cool – it's not, mate you're just a wanker.

Suit manager chain gym wanker will not be impressed with this even more so if he has recently been assaulted by yelling and grunting wanker. So suit wanker will probably ask you to leave if you show up in jeans.

Bonus wankerbility points to be scored by wearing double denim as this look is very hard to pull off, in fact you gain the wankers respect for this. Jeans and denim jacket, it's like the 80's again or was it the summer of 69?

Jeans wanker 5/10 ☐
Double denim wanker 8/10 ☐

26. Long socks wanker

This is usually an older gentlemen's pursuit and helps cover up those unsightly veins. Socks are usually bright white and go to about 2 – 4 inches below the knee dependent on vascularity. Young person long socks wanker is usually a social reject and will always be alone; he may also be wearing sandals with those long socks.

Probably not an ideal training partner unless you have limited options yourself.

Long socks wanker 4/10 ☐

27. Checking your hair wanker

This is an amazing environment for hair checker wanker as wherever you turn in a gym there is a mirror so opportunity a plenty to check your yourself out.

Now some would say you are there to exercise but not for you, it's much more than that, you are also there to look good. Those mirrors aren't there by chance.

In fact, if you're in the middle of using the cable cross, stop what you are doing mid set if a hair is out of place, otherwise those guys behind you laughing (obviously about you, you paranoid wanker) will keep going and you'll never live it down.

If you are training two body parts (for example chest and triceps) then generally speaking say 9 – 12 sets for chest and 7-9 for triceps in total will be up to 21 sets in total. Therefore this offers at least 42 opportunities to check your hair (before and after each set) – fantastic!!

42 looks Hair wanker 7/10 ☐

28. Middle Aged Cap Back to Front Wanker

This is midlife crisis wanker or I'm starting to go bald wanker.

The author can testify to this having tried a variety of headgear in the gym whilst starting my long overdue midlife crisis and none of which looked good at all – I just looked like a douche bag wanker.

The cap back to front when you are 30 or 40 something + just makes you look like an utter wankasaurous but your friends won't tell you as they sympathise with the struggles you are currently going through as it's just a phase so you just carry on looking cool........... mega lol's.

Your wank-fu is weak.

The starting to go bald wanker has the cap glued to his head and is impossible to remove as they live in denial and fear. So this is not just a gym problem, this is their lifestyle problem and the once cool demeanour is now covered in a SWAT cap (Twat) and a department of corrections jacket to try and regain some of their lost youth – "I got in trouble with the cops once, they got my fingerprints!!" Yeah okay buddy so does the posh gym chain you just joined.

Middle aged cap back to front wanker 7/10 ☐
Bald denial wanker 9/10 (embrace the baldness!) ☐

29. Sauna open legs wanker

Now if you're in Austria or Germany or at the local swingers club it is mandatory to remove ones clothes in the sauna; this can be most disconcerting for the uninitiated especially if the people in the sauna were brought up on 70's erotica with enough thatch below to house a family of sparrows.

But in most countries this does not happen but that's not to say that open legs wanker (who's been to Austria) knows how to play this game. He will put his white towel between his legs with legs wide open to give everyone the impression that he is indeed commando. Open legs wanker will revel in your uncomfortable body posture as you discuss the weather and other such yawn a doms, it will get to the point that you make excuses to leave as frankly, you've seen enough and you couldn't give a crap if it rains, if it rains, if it rains on those boys (American Dad joke).

Duly noted that he'll probably then follow you to the spa pool where he becomes smiling spa pool wanker.

Sauna wanker 7/10 ☐
Combined with smiling spa wanker 10/10 ☐

30. Staring at Bums Wanker

Most unfortunate that chain gyms have ranks of cardio equipment so sometimes you are faced with someone's butt right in front of you, now to be fair, you didn't plan this. If you're a man and the gym female fittie is in front of you this is a disaster as this is a no win situation as you don't want to get caught looking at said butt for fear of being known as pervert wanker or out of your league wanker. As such your cardio is short lived as you concentrate more on moving your head around everywhere except directly in front of you or you zone out looking at someone else's butt by accident (and upset them instead), he was not impressed!

If you are a lady and are fortunate enough to have me in your gym and I'm not talking and actually doing something please do look at my trained and buff behind....... I'm not offended at all, if you are a man I'm equally not offended but I'm not "curious" so please don't develop into winking wanker or I become unreasonable wanker.

For the odd exception of a complete tool of a wanker walking around the gym looking at ass this is an uncomfortable development of the chain gym age so we blame them and not much wankerability to be gained here.

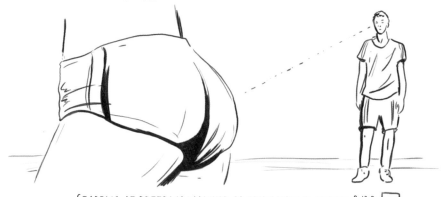

Staring at bottoms wanker as you have no choice 2/10 ☐
Staring at bottoms pervert wanker 10/10 ask them to leave ☐

31. The "I don't want to look like a bodybuilder wanker"

The bane of anyone serious in the fitness and bodybuilding community!!

For some reason civilian non gym users seem to think that a couple of sessions in the gym will create a whole new lifestyle with a brand new physique to match. They've done their research and read Get In Shape magazine or some such like and read an article about how a famous person keeps in shape and it's as easy as that – no, wanker it isn't!

Armed with their new gym vest, towel, water bottle and gloves they complain to the gym instructor after a couple of sessions with no gains, "maybe I need a new programme" or something, "I just don't feel this is working for me".

The most irritating to seasoned gym owners and instructors is the wanker who thinks it's easy, that's why very few succeed and why not many ever get their black belts when they sign up to be the next Jackie Chan.

The same as this raft of 'modern men' (boys) wankers who think if they take steroids they do not have to train.

To complete the look they could also add one of those Bluetooth phone ear pieces to walk around in – you've actually now maxed out your wanker style.

I don't want to look like a bodybuilder after 2 sessions wanker 7/10 ☐
Taking steroids without training 9/10 ☐
Taking steroids without training and having a faded tribal tattoo 10/10 ☐

32. Couples wankers

Now this is an interesting breed as there are a couple that fall into this category (no pun intended):

1. We met in the gym (early days dating) or I'm going to the gym as I want to meet someone.
2. Decided to join the gym together.

1. If you met your perfect person in the gym or are looking for this person, with such a high level of testosterone/pheromones within a short space men and women can display some very odd behaviourisms in order to attract their perfect mate.

Self preening in front of the mirror is important and can be a very useful way of looking in the reflection to see if you are being watched by your prey. For the uninitiated the mirrors are there for these types of reasons.

The mandatory plate slam as you load up the bar will show how strong you are and is very effective in attracting attention.

Make sure if bench pressing to walk around the whole bench first like you are eyeing it up to mate with it – growling a little is an optional extra.

When lifting a little grunt is ok, if you're a screamer this is not cool, frankly - no one likes a screamer despite what you may read.

WHATEVER YOU DO.........NEVER ENGAGE WITH CARDIO VASCULAR EXERCISE! THIS PROMOTES A SWEATY DEMEANOUR AND CAN NEVER EVER LOOK AS GOOD AS DEADLIFTING – KEEP IT HEAVY AND SERIOUS AND IMPRESS WITH WHAT YOU CAN DO.

IF SHE/HE DOES NOT NOTICE WALK OVER AFTERWARDS AND SAY "DID YOU SEE WHAT I JUST DID?" HONESTLY, THIS CANNOT FAIL, IT'S A CLASSIC FLIRTATION OF THE GYM WANKER PROFESSIONAL – GIVE IT A TRY AND SEE HOW YOU GET ON!!! YOU SIMPLY CANNOT FAIL WITH THIS LEVEL OF GAME, THE OPPOSITE SEX WILL LOVE WHAT YOU CAN DO IN THE GYM AND HOW MUCH YOU CAN LIFT, THAT'S A FACT!

IF YOU ARE BODY CONFIDENT, WEAR SHORTS SO SHORT THAT YOU CAN SHOW EVERYONE WHAT YOU HAD FOR LUNCH.

2. SO YOU'RE A COUPLE AND HAVE DECIDED TO JOIN THE GYM TOGETHER!

YES WHY NOT? WHEN YOU'VE BEEN TOGETHER FOR A LITTLE WHILE THOSE CALORIES BURNT AT HOME SEEM TO BECOME MUCH LESS AS THE WEEKS PASS BY – DON'T THEY?

Classic wank couples formations include –

- His and her matching training gear, also wear gloves because that's cool.
- If you have money you could get state of the art training clothing from an expensive brand – it's best to go for the most outrageous colours you can get and in this case be polar opposites, for example, if one is bright green the other should be bright orange etc but make sure it's expensive!!
- Share a locker to save the deposit money – good thinking and also allows you to talk outside the opposite sex changing room for ages about who's got what towel or where did you leave the dog etc – absolutely nobody minds this at all – it's cool, honest.
- Talk aimlessly for ages around the machines so no-one else can use them, in fact if you're married use this opportunity to talk far more than you ever do at home together, in fact talk loads of utter bollocks ensuring that no one else can use the machines.
- Have an argument as one is caught checking someone else out – this is classic couple wank territory right here and at least everyone else reaps the benefit of this (insecure wanker).
- If you walk around the gym like a pair of lost puppies, giving not one single exercise a fairly decent go or showing any interest it is clear to everyone that you are missionary position couple wankers – go on experiment and do something different, don't be a wankerpussy. Maybe experiment with a sitting preacher curl, the excitement of something different will feel like the first time you did anal.........so I'm told.
- If you have one of those rare loving relationships you can pat each other for no reason on the bottom and laugh together loudly and other such things – the gym membership really love this!!! "Ahhh, look at those pair they look so happy" – this is EXACTLY what everyone is thinking you in love wankers.

Couples Wankers 3/10 Couples ☐
wankers hogging the machines 7/10 ☐
Jealous Rowing checking out asses couple Wankers 9/10 ☐

33. Phone Wanker

These guys............yes these piss ass guys!!

Let's be really clear here – we don't give an absolute shit for your life and what is going on with it. We are gym people, completely self absorbed and have no time for your crap so we don't want to hear it.

If you are someone who has to text or check your social media when in the gym, you are either not training properly or you are so insecure that you haven't got enough likes to your 'check in' status at the gym – seriously, why do people check themselves in a the gym? We couldn't give a crap, shake it up a little and check yourself in at a strip club – ladies, you'll get more followers!

If you are part of some Special Forces outfit or are on call for an International incident then ok, keep your phone on in the gym, if not get rid of it and never, ever answer a call!

If you are the phone guy/girl who walks around pressing buttons or speaking to people in the gym you are a wanker.

ONLY 3 LIKES TO MY GYM CHECK-IN STATUS??

Phone Wanker 8/10

GETTING YOU OWN BACK ON PHONE WANKER

Fortunately there are ways of fighting back against the phone wanker.

If you work in a gym or know the gym people suggest music volume increase immediately to the max, ideally select Slayer, Napalm Death or One Direction to clear him/her and their phone out the gym with immediate effect.

You could also walk around behind them dropping random plates on the floor. Use the cleaning spray (the one that sweaty wanker never uses) and add some random trajectory shots their way – they'll soon get the message.

Ask couples wankers to stand next to them throughout the duration of the call as they discuss this weekend's missionary position.

Engage winking wanker to make contact with a smile (usually works but these are usually confined to the changing room).

It's time for the weekly/monthly fire alarm test and don't allow them back in afterwards (for their safety).

Earn some wankerbility yourself by the following:

Engaging couples wanker/winking wanker 7/10 ☐
Getting Slayer/Napalm Death played 8/10 ☐
Getting One Direction Played. Go home and don't ever come back ☐

34. Selfie Wanker

Most gym wankers are guilty of this particular wank manoeuvre the most.

The selfie, often referred to by parents on social media as "the only time I ever see my children" has consumed gym go-ers for the last decade.

Not a gym session goes by without observing a selfie wanker, the most perturbing are those that do it in the changing room – seriously stop this please, it puts you off your protein shake more than winking wanker eyeing you up.

Serious gym goers aren't very impressed with the selfie wanker so always make sure that your path is clear behind otherwise the photo bomb will happen usually in the form of a middle digit being offered your way.

Make sure the mandatory selfie styling is in place – for the gym this includes:

1. Hair perfect (again, a non-cardio day)
2. Hold the waist in
3. Do a few sets on biceps even though it was chest day to get a little pump
4. Ensure your pout is perfect (this is for men and women)
5. Make sure you applied fake tan the night before, no-one likes pasty skin wanker
6. Show the brand you are wearing! Very important for credibility or getting free stuff from the new type clothing brand
7. Have a leg machine in the background for effect – you have to find this first......it will probably be in the corner

Selfie wanker 6/10 ☐

35. Instagram wanker

We all love a bit of social media and Instagram, it is the perfect way to stalk your favourite fitness inspirations and watch all sorts of videos of them doing new bizarre routines on the gym equipment. Great, give it a go, of course you will look as hot as them using the abductor machine standing up to work your butt right? Wrong, it's more than likely that the newbie Instagram wanker will forget the exercise they were so desperate to try yesterday and end up sitting on the machine becoming a phone wanker as they try to relocate said video.

So once you have re-learnt what you were meant to be doing you give it a go only to find it looked a lot easier in the video and that your balance is not what you thought it would be.

Instagram wankers are usually more women than men, so if you spot one on the squat rack thrusting her fanny into the air do not let ladies man wanker anywhere near her, she's not sending out signals she's just mastering the latest trend.

Instagram wanker 7/10 ☐

36. Kardashian wanker

Kardashian wanker is predominantly female. Big butts are big news apparently and as most gym wankers don't have the dollar to buy a butt, they decide to build one.

Kardashian wanker will always be found by the squat rack, she may occasionally make a visit to the leg press but first she needs to do all the squats. Usually dressed in short shorts so she can take a sly look in the mirrors to see the progress of that bubble butt.

The seasoned Kardashian wanker will actually have good form and be able to squat more than any leg day wanker and that's not surprising as she will squat for at least an hour 5 times a week so you probably wouldn't want to rush her to use the rack or she may squat you instead. The newbie Kardashian wanker will hog that Smith machine, and usually does not add more than a 5kg plate each side only squatting to a 45 degree angle, some will give up after they feel the DOMs the next day and go on eBay to buy a pair of knickers with padding in the butt and try to pass these off as their ass well earned!

Seasoned Kardashian wanker 3/10 ☐
Newbie Kardashian wanker 7/10 ☐
Padded pants wanker 8/10 ☐
Being married to Kayne West 10/10 ☐

37. Clicky wankers

Often found in classes or huddled in corners of the gym; clicky wankers always come in groups or pairs. They are more concerned about gossip than an actual workout and they come in two forms.

1. Middle aged clicky lady wankers

These wankers only ever go to classes and always turn up 30 minutes early to have a chat about the school run, TV soaps, and that bitch Carol. They are always very pally with the person teaching the class and like to tell all the instructors that their classes are the best, everyone else is useless. They have a spot where they ALWAYS exercise, God forbid they would have to jog on the spot anywhere else (It's like they've marked their territory.....like a poodle would).

At the end of the class they always stand in the middle of the corridor to finish their chat about how busy their week is and the million things they have to do.....blah blah.

It is important to remember not to try to engage conversation with these ladies if you are not born and bred locally, this will take time. You probably need to bring cakes or something, this is known as a bribe or dependent on who you are talking to as flirtation, failing that you will be shot down in flames and never be accepted.

AFTER THE
SCHOOL RUN

2. Young lad clicky wankers

These young men usually come in threes and spend their time in the free weights section and take it in turns, one does the exercise, one spots and one takes pictures and then uploads to some sort of social media, usually with hash tags like #lads #beastmode #gymlife #yawn.

They do not interact with other people in the gym although they do talk loud enough so everyone can hear what good banter they have and how Parsons (I can only assume this is a surname) got wrecked at the weekend, the club was LIT and Dan shagged a wrong'un up an alleyway. Clicky young lad wankers are usually found in the pub after their workout telling everyone how they have hit their new (exaggerated) personal best. Ladies if this is unclear..........they are not a catch!

Middle aged clicky lady wanker 8/10 ☐
Young lad clicky wanker 10/10 ☐

38. Go to the gym twice in January wanker

So you're fed up of the lard or getting out of breath from walking to the pizza place so this New Year you are sorting it, no more excuses we are DOING THIS! (Said like Joe from Family Guy).

Being a member of a gym for some wankers is almost kudos like, "my gym is better than yours" or if you're really a kudos asshole "my country club is better than yours".

If you're not really serious about it, don't select the spit and sawdust gym; find a commercial one with nice towels, free soap in the shower, loads of personal trainers and a bar for a low calorie vodka afterwards.

So you part with your yearly membership fee at the commercial chain gym which could buy you a small ranch in a different country, have a free coffee with mandatory biscuit (or was that fake tan wanker walking past?) and you are there the very next day!

Excited with the prospect of turning your life around you are most upset that the coffee isn't free anymore thereafter and the low calorie vodka is served with full fat coke. What is this shenanigans?? The gym social events are as dull as dish water and usually involve some form of exercise instead of a bar crawl, club 18 – 30 its not!

So you go twice, unhappy with the results and the fact that you did one sit up so why are you still fat? So you decide to call it a day and get a social life instead – however, if you are single and are involved with online dating make sure you mention that you are a member of the gym – kudos to you!!

January Wanker 1/10 ☐

39. Start my diet next week wanker

Well if you are a competitive athlete nothing gets in the way, it's known as focus, everything else and everyone else can smoke a large one.

For the rest of us non-athlete people unlike you we have weekends and stuff so we can't live like that. Even Jenny bitch face has a party going on that I need to get to and although she's a wasteless and tasteless mess she's part of the scene so I must show. So upon showing up those canapés look really good and the fake Champagne (Prosecco, for the great unwashed) and typical for Jenny, is too good to turn away. If you show up with your little plastic container with your boiled chicken with shreds of broccoli and asking for it to be heated up frankly, not cool...........Seriously, she showed up to my party with broccoli?? Welcome to being a social pariah, the diet thing is not cool.

Fact is, if you are not a competitor life gets in the way, if you are a competitor you have no life. To quote Tom Hanks on his social media "sometimes I'm in shape, sometimes I'm not, but you've got to live a little". Too true gym wankers.

Start the diet next week 3/10 ☐
Say it every week for 52 weeks a year 10/10 (standard) ☐

WANK CHAPTER 3
Commercial Chain Gym Wankers

40. Reception wanker

If you've bothered your ass to get out of your warm bed on a cold morning and want to brave the gym at 6am (knowing that you are going to bump into football/political wanker afterwards) you sure as hell would like a hello when you bother to show up!

The minnow gyms will make a point to get to know their membership as their very livelihoods depend on it. This can often get lost in the commercial chain gym environment.

Showing up at commercial gym without even a "hello" from reception wanker actually hurts, it really does! I was in bed and forced myself to come here and you can't even be bothered to break your morning conversation with cleaning wanker to acknowledge my custom? Even worse, you're on your social media checking meaningless stuff so I'm sorry I interrupted you because I'm a committed morning wanker.

Reception wanker may also control the 'gates' to get in and bizarrely some gyms now have fingerprint recognition as an id system to get in!!?? Last time I gave anyone my fingerprints was when I was unreasonable wanker and people in uniform wanted to have a chat with me (law enforcement wankers).

To shake things up a bit you could of course ask Lady Duffolcote-Hugh Grant from the ladies formation juggling team for a drink afterwards? And then covertly clone her fingerprint from the glass of fizz you've just bought her so when going through Customs (sorry the gym entrance) you could lay down the clone on the scanner so her face appears on the screen above, as in Mission Impossible as you get in!! But then you remember that you've paid your yearly membership so nothing is gained; Tom Cruise you ain't and all you've done is broken into the gym you're a member of for a free workout or a catch up in the sauna with open legs wanker. You could of course try getting a free protein bar on her account maybe, but a session with masseuse wanker is unlikely as he'll probably guess that something is amiss when you show up using her name.

Rude and bored chain Gym Reception Wankers 9/10 ☐

41. Big Jeremy wanker

Curious isn't it that I attended a ladies only gym one time (for a job interview) and all the ladies showing up at the gym greeted the male receptionist by way of "hello big Jeremy"??, every lady said it like it was a mandatory ruling on their membership cards. Now Jeremy didn't look to me like he'd done a day's workout in his life, unless I wasn't paying enough attention to something else he was in possession of. Big Jeremy you are a legend.

If you are addressed by the ladies in such a way you have earned maximum wank points.

Big Jeremy, make your gym members call you Big Jeremy wanker 10/10 ☐

42. Commercial music gym wankers

Whatever happened to individual music in the gym? Where's the metal? Where is the drum and bass? If that's not your thing you can at least have some appreciation for some AC/DC in the gym at least??

You don't?? Well wanker the collapse of motivational gym music is your fault! In some commercial gym chains who pay for their licensed music now they are told what they have to play (no requests please) often controlled by reception wanker, all the music is too safe as you don't want anyone offended!

Bullet in the head by Rage Against The Machine motivated a gym generation but now nowhere to be seen with commercial gym chain wankers.

If you are involved in music selection for gym chains grow a pair and remove One Direction as this is not gym music, it's shit music.

Commercial music gym wankers 9/10 bring back the noise!! ☐

43. Commercial gym crap food wankers

Now in the old days you would have a choice of a protein drink after your workout or a baked potato if it's a posh place.

Nowadays; commercial gym will offer you a selection of food but who the hell puts together the menu and thinking behind these?

Often very little healthy food to be found it's just an expensive crap 'restaurant' – they'll offer you free wifi as an incentive - wooooo.

The commercial gym crap food restaurant is often found next to the entrance of the gym and someone thought it would be absolute genius to serve bacon sandwiches on the menu. So as you arrive you smell bacon, as you leave you smell bacon – bravo chain gym wankers for your lack of vision – I'll get a beer with that please.

Crap food wankers 8/10 ☐
Bacon smelling gym 10/10 ☐

44. The no exercise personal training wanker

What the hell happened here exactly? The personal training game has become flooded over the last few years, far removed from my days as an unqualified instructor teaching everything I knew....ahem.

But it stands to rights if you are paying for 'knowledge' you really want it from someone who looks like they practice their knowledge – if you can't be bothered to do it yourself then why do I want to be taught or bother my ass to be told by you to "get down and give me 20"?

Now this is not an insult to the accomplished personal trainers out there as non training personal training wanker upsets them as well, you don't have to be Thor wanker or Wonder Woman wanker to personal train, but at least you look like you do a bit wanker.

The no exercise personal training wanker 9/10 Practise what you preach! ☐

45. I'M A MASSEUSE AND AVAILABLE FOR HOME VISITS WANKER

WELL AS PART OF THE COMMERCIAL GYM CHAIN, YOU CAN GET EXTRAS AND BY THAT I MEAN TREATMENT OF YOUR INJURIES AS WELL AS THE ON HAND ODD BALL LOOKING MASSEUSE WANKER.

PLAY THIS ONE CAREFULLY AND CHECK OUT SAID MASSEUSE CREDENTIALS FIRST JUST IN CASE SHORT SHORTS WANKER HAS SLIPPED INTO THE ROOM BEFORE MASSEUSE WANKER COULD GET THERE.

IF IN TALK WITH MASSEUSE WANKER AND THE MENTION OF HOME VISITS COME UP IN CONVERSATION AND NOT PROMPTED BY YOU, YOU HAVE AN ENTIRELY DIFFERENT WANKER ON YOUR HANDS.....OR ARE YOU IN HIS?

HE MAY ALSO BE IN CONTROL OF THE SUN BEDS AND OF COURSE WILL RECOMMEND ONE FOR YOU, IF IT'S IN THE SAME ROOM AS HIS MASSAGE BED HE MAY OFFER TO ADJUST THE CONTROLS FOR YOU AND HE THEN BECOMES VERY ATTENTIVE WANKER.

DODGY MASSEUSE WANKER 9/10
OFFERS A SUN BED AS WELL 10/10

46. Virtual wankers

Imagine showing up at the minnow gym for your aerobics class and there is no instructor! – You what mate?

So the money making gym chain wankers in their wisdom thought what a great idea it would be to have virtual instruction – yes that's right, watch a fucking video.

So what is the point of this gym I'm paying for exactly? Let's quickly recap:

1. Reception wanker is a wanker
2. Music is from wanktown records
3. I arrive at the gym smelling good, I leave smelling of bacon
4. Manager is a suit wanker
5. Personal trainers don't look like they train wankers
6. The coffee (or vodka) isn't free – utter conning wankers

And now you don't have an instructor – case closed the death of the gym has arrived.

I'll check if someone from the latest reality TV show has just released a fitness DVD and stay at home instead.

Virtual wankers (maximise our shareholders very short-lived profits) 10/10 □

WANK CHAPTER 4
CHANGING ROOMS

47. The Donald Trump hair manoeuvre

This is an advanced level wanker manoeuvre and rarely can be attempted with any notable success by younger men.

First you need to have a thatch of hair mass, however there also needs to be a vacant spot in the middle of your head, this is similar to in denial going bald wanker.

After showering you need to apply a considerable quantity of hair mousse (about half a can's worth each time) to try and resurrect what clearly is dying in the centre surrounds of your head. Hair drying time is approximately 30 minutes but can take longer. With such a considerable effort the fuse blowing in the hairdryer happens regularly, when this does happen proceed to the next one available provided by the gym, no problem, you don't pay for them.

This can be a tricky situation as hairy bollocks wanker will need those dangling bad boys drying soon so try and time your hair manoeuvre perfectly; hairy balls wanker does not take too kindly to being damp bollocks in pants wanker and can become unreasonable naked wanker very quickly.

After approximately 30 minutes remove hairdryer and obtain portable hand mirror, you should be now be able to comb over the longer plump bits of hair over the soon to be banished bald spot – this is the Donald Trump hair manoeuvre wanker.

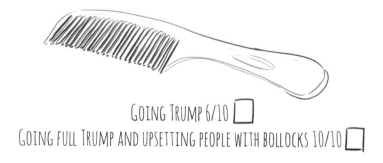

Going Trump 6/10 ☐
Going full Trump and upsetting people with bollocks 10/10 ☐

48. The football political wanker

So if you are giving consideration to a very annoying twat of a wanker it is football/political wanker.

Not everyone can pull this off as you need to have a serious lack of social skills coupled with a noxious voice that grates the eardrums of anyone in close proximity; also it's standard to conduct or address your audience being completely naked, this is an unusual skill set and it must be carried out with no qualms whatsoever. Football political wanker will look you square in the eyes as his dingle dangle swings in the breeze.

So reception wanker has upset you already and then as you go to enter the changing room and before you open the door you can hear his droning uninteresting voice already, not the best start.

If the gym is busy this is regrettable as you can bet your life the only lockers that are available are the ones close to him.

There are only 2 topics of conversation, everything else is meaningless:

1. Football
2. Politics

Football is not for everyone and for this reason that's why this guy is such a wanker; he can't talk quietly and he will have some football knowledge, however, if you bizarrely wish to submit your view it will be shot down immediately – he is king of this naked castle.

If he's not whining on about some 'shocking' performance and then saying "well I knew that was going to happen" he'll shake up the conversation with some random political genius viewpoints.

Politics cannot and should not be discussed naked at any time, the thought of our politicians being naked is enough to put you off your protein brownie so cut that shit out. Also politics cannot be won or lost in the gym changing room so seriously football/ political wanker do everyone a favour and shut the fuck up!

His political views are often ignorant and have never been really thought through and are basic to mid level politics at best. These misguided and ill-judged comments makes you want to lose your rag with him but you don't for fear of engaging in conversation with him. You feel anxious around him and he makes you feel a little ill because you want to tell him so bad to shut up, but if you do whether he likes it or not from that day on he has you, you are conversation buddy and your life will never be the same again – he'll probably use the personal trainer's surveillance skills to find out where you live.

Football/Political wanker will be on hand ready to hold court everyday with anyone who is prepared to listen to them.

Football/Political wanker 10/10 ☐
Having the inner strength to ignore football/
political wanker without resorting to violence 11/10 ☐

49. PROTEIN WANKER

IT'S VITALLY IMPORTANT POST WORKOUT THAT YOU HAVE YOUR PROTEIN SHAKE AS SOON AS POSSIBLE, IF NOT EVERYTHING YOU'VE JUST DONE IS AN UTTER WASTE OF TIME, THAT'S NOT GOSSIP, THAT'S SCIENCE.

YOU HAVE APPROXIMATELY 120 SECONDS FROM DOWNTIME TO GET TO THE CHANGING ROOM FOR YOUR PREPARED PROTEIN DRINK. ONCE LOCKER IS OPENED YOU CAN USUALLY SPEND ABOUT 5-10 SECONDS IN FLIRTATION WITH SAID PROTEIN DRINK IN ITS FINERY DEPENDENT ON HOW HARD YOU'VE JUST WORKED. GIVE IT A LITTLE SHAKE OR A GENTLE STROKE OF THE BOTTLE LIKE YOU ARE GETTING IT EXCITED.

THEN WITHOUT WARNING NAIL IT AS QUICK AS YOU CAN WITHOUT MERCY!! IT'S MANDATORY TO LET OUT AN "AHHHHHH" AS SOON AS YOU'RE DONE SO EVERYONE HEARS YOUR COMPLETION OF WORKOUT IS OVER AND IT ALSO INFORMS EVERYONE AROUND YOU THAT YOUR MUSCLE GROWTH HAS COMMENCED; IMPORTANT TO LET OUT THE SAME NOISE YOU MAKE WHEN YOU'VE HAD A TROUBLESOME FART THAT REFUSES TO GIVE IN OR IF YOU ARE RELATIONSHIP WANKER AND YOU ARE HAVING YOUR ONCE A MONTH SEXUAL MISSIONARY TIME.

AFTERWARDS REMOVE PROTEIN SHAKE CONTAINER FROM MOUTH AND WITH ONE FINGER JUST DAB THAT BIT THAT MISSED YOUR MOUTH LIKE YOUR FAVOURITE PORN STAR.

WANKER-BAR

PROTEIN WANKER 4/10 ☐
PORN STAR PROTEIN WANKER 7/10 ☐

50. Bleeding Wanker

You've pushed yourself to the vertical limit with your training and in doing so you may consider yourself as athlete status, if so you may not be a wanker after all and if that's the case you've wasted your money buying this book. You may wish to reconsider your serious approach to training as everyone is some form of wanker, you must find your path.

But whilst vomiting wanker can earn some wanker gains by showing everyone a projectile reminder of the previous night, bleeding wanker lives in the present.

So before you go to the docs because your nose is bleeding where you've burst some sort of blood vessel you decide to leave your blood on the changing room floor — this is gross wanker, doesn't matter who you are.

Worse is the person who has trained legs to the max and trained those glutes hard. Sat down in the changing room afterwards now being protein wanker, unbeknown to them a little blood pool is left on the bench behind them when they get up — this is piles wanker, not cool but I guess that means you've pushed your shit to the max.

CLEAN IT UP

Nose bleed leave mess on the floor wanker 9/10 ☐
Piles wanker 10/10 ☐

51. Gear wanker

Every gym has a minimum of one gear wanker but sometimes they can be by the dozen. So the use of steroids within the training environment is hardly earth shattering news and conversation usually remains confined to the changing rooms.

Discussion of different types of gear and gear combinations is commonplace and for the uninitiated can be a little intimidating. That's not to say it happens openly at every gym and less so at posh chain gyms.

Knowledgeable gear wanker has been in the game for some years and over time usually has become more circumspect with open conversation in front of civilian non users. The one to watch is the young type gear wanker that has overloaded on testosterone whose ego develops at the same rate as his guns; he's now a know-all in the training environment, a sporting maverick.

Watch him leave in his wanker chariot after training.

Gear wanker 1/10 (comes with the territory) ☐
Young gear wanker know it all 7/10 ☐
With a wanker chariot and go faster stripes 10/10 ☐

52. Shoulder hair wanker

This is an odd wanker, a very odd wanker in fact.

When you look in the mirror can you not see those massive hairs sticking up from the top of your shoulders in their curly finery? It doesn't matter if you are dark haired, grey or even if you inherited the ginger gene; in the gym and after the shower they gleam, in fact you glow more than the last time the death star was destroyed shortly before the Ewok's were eradicated by mad cows disease. We can all see this and don't want to, how come you don't or maybe you embrace the woolly mammoth look?

Now in the 70's when porn was kinda un-talked about but cool nevertheless you would have blended right in as body hair was rife in those days as razors had not been invented, the cave man era was only a decade before at the same time when someone had the flawed idea of making the dinosaurs extinct? Never got that, they would have made great pets, just like the Ewok's would have – it's a shame really.

Shoulder hair wanker 7/10 ☐
Ginger shoulder hair wanker 10/10 ☐
(it's like reflective pubes on your shoulders)

53. Hair drying back hair wanker

So you think the shoulder hair grunting ape like Neanderthal is unusual? Meet hairy back need to dry my back hair wanker.

It's like your worst Greek holiday gone wrong; remember being on the beach and Borat walks over in his mankini to say hi? (Okay Borat was not Greek but you get the picture). Back hair is NOT attractive, it isn't, if you think otherwise you are reading the wrong type of women's magazines.

There is nothing attractive about back hair unless you've joined some sort of 'specialist' dating service (weird and single really need to get laid wanker).

So it's an uncomfortable surprise to gym folk (especially the newbies) when in the changing room that back hair wanker takes hold of the hair dryer and dries his back – they seem to do it with such pride as well almost like they are teen wolf.

Worse still if they are in possession of a comb and try to wrap their arm around their back to comb their back hair.......the author can attest to seeing this horrific sight........

Drying back hair wanker is a grizzly sight and if they are naked chances are they are also shoulder hair wanker which means also very hairy butt crack wanker.

It's at that moment you remember that you are paying to be here.

Hair drying back hair wanker 7/10 ☐
Naked with fluff everywhere wanker 10/10 ☐

54. Pubes wanker

Now most of us these days keep our thatch in fairly good order but that's not to say that everyone does – does that include you?

Getting into the shower or when walking barefoot around the changing room is a bit like dodge the pubes. But you know, there will always be one little fucker that finds a way. You notice this when you go to bed in the evening and take your socks off to find one little curly pube just stuck right there on your big toe. You need to be careful here as if you're a bit of a player this is a really bad way of transporting different colour pubes into your bed by complete accident. Sometimes you just can't explain these things in an entirely logical manner or rather a believable story.

Player or not or if you are in a committed relationship trying to explain there are different colour pubes in the bed and your explanation is that they must have stuck to your feet after showering in the gym could open up a complete different level of complexity in your relationship.

Also pubes wanker can be the same problem as hairy back wanker in liking to keep things healthy and dry, as such there will always be some loose ones. As soon as that hair dryer takes to the pubes mound as well as penis and balls moving in the direction away from the dryer there can also be a concoction of pubes of different sizes leaving the body and could be heading in your direction. If you are thatch hairy bollocks wanker and the guy to the side you don't like, this is your time, make it count!

Hair dryer pubes wanker distributor 6/10 ☐
Showering your enemy with your pubes 8/10 ☐
Causing a couple to have relationship counselling as
an affair is suspected because of your pubes 10/10 ☐

55. Toenail clippings wanker

If vomiting wanker has any uncertainly on making good from their night before, bring them into the changing room to watch this social disgrace wanker. If you are reading this and you take toenail clippers into the changing rooms with you, you are a horrible little wanker.

Keeping clean, yes, clipping your toenails and then leaving them on the floor after you've gone for others to walk on...........gross!

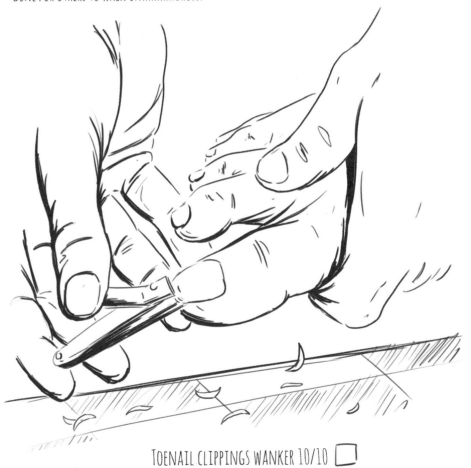

Toenail clippings wanker 10/10 ☐

56. Doesn't pay for lockers — tight ass wanker

The gym is busy so there will be little space to find a locker but how many times do you open one to find it full of someone's gear?

Gym lockers are very cheap, you get your money back and if you make the effort to go to the gym and don't have change chances are you are broke wanker.

Doesn't pay for lockers wanker 4/10 ☐
Asking pubes wanker to shower their gear with curls 10/10 ☐

57. Naked old wanker

It must be when you retire that you lose all your inhibitions along with your marbles and that you have no fear or concern whatsoever as to who sees you in the buff. Whether you are in good shape or not you don't give an absolute shit what anyone thinks (maybe not such a bad thing actually!).

This is not the grumpy old wanker from the village wanker this is an age thing where there is a cut off switch where you just don't care anymore.

Naked old wanker may not even know you but will come over with floppy bollocks swinging and ask you how your day is, no towel in hand of course, he doesn't need one as he's not used the gym yet.

This is tricky because 9 times out of 10 they are not being pervert wanker they just want a chat, albeit it a naked one. But if you engage in conversation and his mates show up you are now trapped and within a matter of minutes you can be surrounded by a dozen cocks and bollocks of varying sizes and floppy man boobs. There will always be one who puts one leg up on the bench to allow his family jewels to swing, now not knowing where to look you are now watching the pubes on the floor instead.

If you are below the age of 30 this can be a very uncomfortable situation and you can develop into sweaty wanker very quickly, gear wanker will be nowhere to be seen to assist you. Thor wanker left long ago as he sees these situations developing and makes good his escape. Short shorts wanker is in the ladies changing room wearing a ladies wig so effectively you are all alone.

Good luck.

Naked old wanker (they all do it) 3/10
Getting naked yourself to blend in 1/10 not advised ☐

58. The Winking Wanker

So in the gym you have the staring at bum's wanker but in the changing room it is the winking wanker. If this has never happened to you, you are clearly an ugly wanker, intimidating wanker or very small penis wanker.

The winking wanker is usually subtle at first and waits like a praying mantis ready to strike, this will usually be as your pants are about to be removed or something such like and they give you that double look, even if your eyes meet theirs accidently (or was it an accident??) this is usually followed by a wink to gauge interest. This is usually from older men not aware that winking was from a bygone age, they are probably also married.

If they've misjudged your demeanour this can sometimes result in bloody winking hospitalised wanker.

Winking wanker 10/10 ☐

59. Cheap aftershave/deodorant wanker

If you are the sort of person who goes to the gym to impress you have fallen foul of many of the wankerism's within this definitive wanker guide.

So we don't expect everything to be smelling of roses and Gucci, that's not really the thing here. It's the behaviour of some, once they have trained who cover themselves in smelly horrible shit and in doing so cover themselves head to toe.

You pollute the changing room worse than farting wanker who smiles and says "better out than in" – very original! It's also important to add additional talc to your private areas and leave a load on the floor behind you which highlights where toenail wanker was earlier. Deodorant wanker will also pay no attention to his surrounds and happily spray the person behind them like a dog pissing in the corner to mark his territory.

You utter wanker.

Cheap aftershave/deodorant wanker 6/10 ☐
Pissing your deodorant over other people 10/10 ☐

60. Grower not a shower wanker

This is the polar opposite to naked old wanker and it's not penis envy wanker either. This is usually young person who has clearly never had a prostrate check yet and is terrified of being seen naked in front of others especially if things are on the 'cold' side.

So changing becomes technically difficult. If you've just got out the shower you need to tie that towel around yourself so tight that you start to lose circulation in everything below your legs (you're not helping yourself here by the way) you must have a towel long enough that you can dry yourself without having to remove it, in fact you need the tent of towels.

Once dry it's then very tricky to get your clothes back on with a towel on your waist tighter that the local vicar's daughter's chastity belt (granted dependent on where you grew up). This takes practice and best to do this at home first so the procedure is seamless, any mistakes and it can be very embarrassing.

If you have any uncertainty best to use a private cubicle and then people will just say you are a small dick wanker anyway and accept your fate.

Naked old wankers can intimidate you to the point that you don't like the gym any more.

Being intimidated by naked old wanker 8/10 ☐
Falling over because you lose circulation in your legs 10/10 ☐

A Conclusion Of Wank-Ageddon

So many wankers, so little time.

60 wankers have been identified here but there are more, way much more; in fact we are only just scratching the tip of the wankoff.

If you have been affected by anything in this book or if you have a wanker style that you would like to 'bring to the surface' or have observed wanky behaviour, please do email us at wanker@gymwanker.com or post on our Gym Wankers social media scoreboard (You phone wanker you).

The gym is a community but wankers are everywhere. Enjoy your gym time and improve those wanker gains.

Farewell until next time.